Science Tools

Microscopes

by Adele Richardson

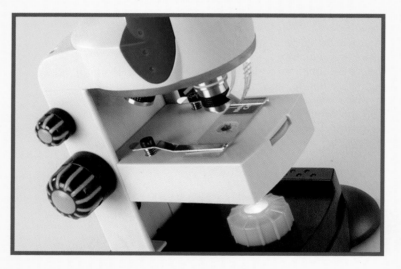

Consultant:
Dr. Ronald Browne
Associate Professor of Elementary Education
Minnesota State University, Mankato

Capstone *press*

Mankato, Minnesota

First Facts is published by Capstone Press
151 Good Counsel Drive, P.O. Box 669, Mankato, Minnesota 56002
www.capstonepress.com

Library of Congress Cataloging-in-Publication Data
Richardson, Adele, 1966–
    Microscopes / by Adele Richardson.
    p. cm.—(First facts. Science tools)
    Summary: Introduces the function, parts, and uses of microscopes, and provides
instructions for two activities that demonstrate how a microscope works.
    Includes bibliographical references (p. 23).
    ISBN 0-7368-2517-7 (hardcover)
    1. Microscopes—Juvenile literature. [1. Microscopes.] I. Title. II. Series.
QH211.R43 2004
502'.8'2—dc22   2003013400

Editorial Credits

Christopher Harbo, editor; Juliette Peters, designer; Erin Scott/SARIN Creative, illustrator;
    Scott Thoms, illustrator; Deirdre Barton, photo researcher; Eric Kudalis, product
    planning editor

Photo Credits

Capstone Press/Gary Sundermeyer, 1, 4, 5, 6, 7, 9, 12, 16, 18
Capstone Press/GEM Photo Studio/Dan Delaney, cover
Corbis/Clouds Hill Imaging Ltd., 11; Lester V. Bergman, 14; Ron Boardman/Frank Lane Pictu
    Agency, 13 (right); Roger Ressmeyer, 20; Royalty–Free, 15
Photo Researchers Inc./Science Photo Library/Andrew Syred, 13 (left); Astrid & Hanns-Frieder
    Michler, 17

Table of Contents

The Class Investigates

Mrs. Arkin's class is looking for **microbes** in water. A microbe is a living thing that can only be seen with a microscope.

The students put a drop of pond water on a **slide**. They put tap water on another slide. The students look at each slide under a microscope.

Turn to page 19 to try this activity!

What Is a Microscope?

A microscope is a tool that makes small things look larger. A microscope shows people details that are too small to see with human eyes.

Microscopes can make things look 100, 200, or 400 times larger. This student is looking at sand with a microscope.

 **Fun Fact:**
Microbes are the smallest living creatures on Earth.

Parts of a Microscope

A microscope has many parts. The tube holds the lenses. The **stage** holds a slide. Focus knobs move the stage up and down to make images clear. A lamp under the stage shines light through the slide.

Fun Fact:
Scientists believe Hans and Zacharias Janssen invented the first microscope with two lenses in 1590.

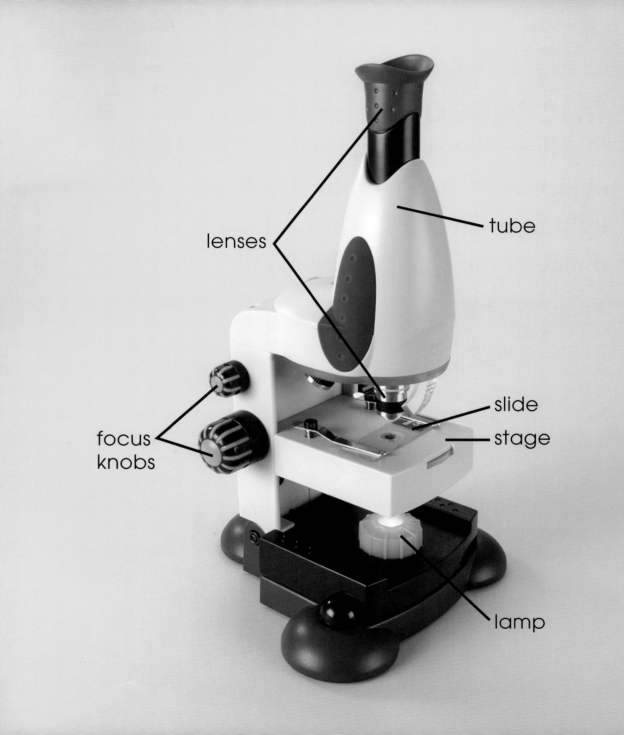

lenses

tube

slide

stage

focus
knobs

lamp

9

Microscope Lenses

Microscopes use curved lenses to make objects look larger. **Objective lenses** collect light from an object. They send a larger image of the object to the **eyepiece lenses**.

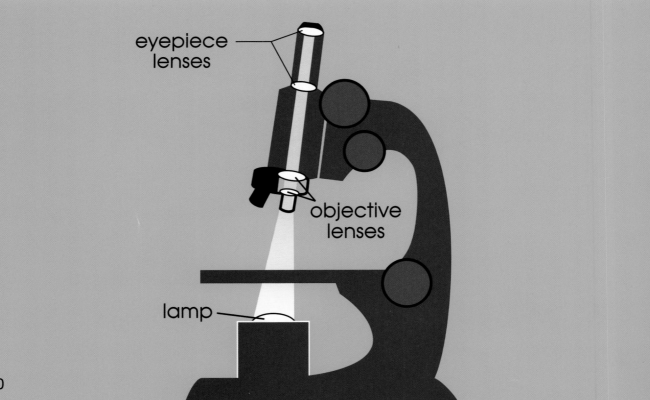

eyepiece lenses

objective lenses

lamp

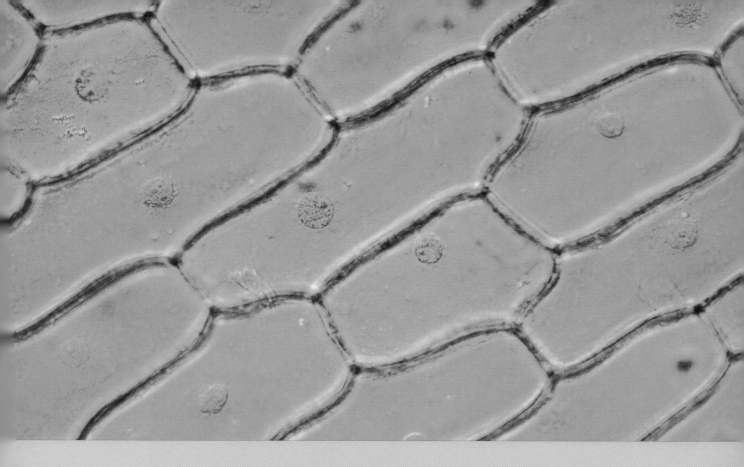

The eyepiece lenses **magnify** the image of the object again. This onion skin looks 200 times larger through the eyepiece lenses.

Microscopes in School

Students use microscopes to compare materials. This student is looking at cotton and silk **fibers**. The fibers look the same without a microscope.

Cotton and silk fibers look different under a microscope. The silk looks like tubes of glass. The cotton looks like crinkled ribbon.

Silk   Cotton

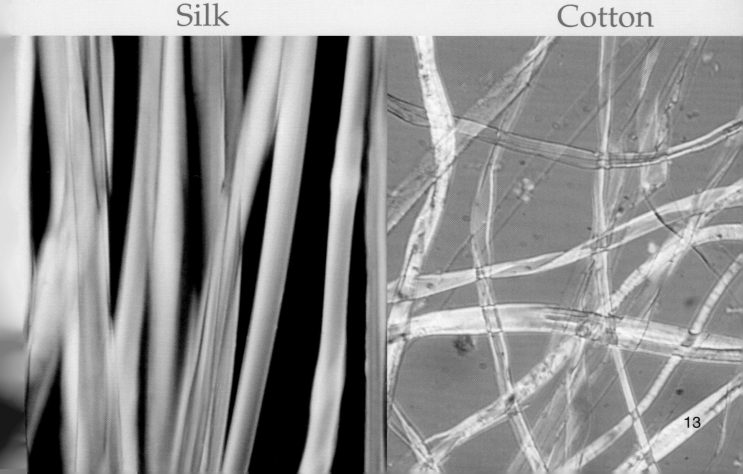

Other Uses for Microscopes

Microscopes are used to study blood. Blood has red cells and white cells. White cells fight infection. A person with a high number of white blood cells may be sick.

red blood cells

white blood cell

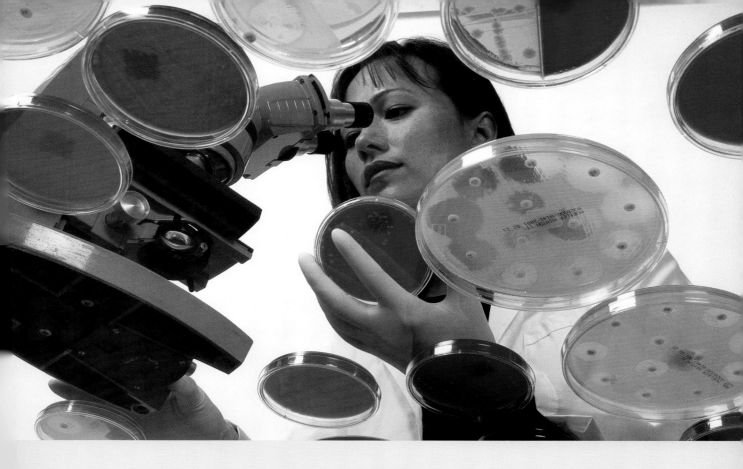

Scientists use microscopes to study living things. Scientists study life in pond and ocean water. They also use microscopes to study germs.

Salt and sugar look alike when spilled on a table. But they taste very different. Do they look the same under a microscope? Let's find out!

Try It!

What You Need

2 slides
salt
sugar
microscope

salt

What You Do

1. Place a few grains of salt on a microscope slide.
2. Place a few grains of sugar on another slide.
3. Carefully set the slide with the salt on the microscope stage. Look at the salt under the microscope.
4. Focus the microscope until you can see the salt clearly.
5. Remove the slide from the stage.
6. Set the microscope slide with the sugar on the stage. Look at the sugar through the microscope.

What are the differences between the salt and the sugar?

What Did They Learn?

Mrs. Arkin's class wanted to see if pond water had more microbes in it than tap water. Which water do you think held more microbes?

Try It!

What You Need

2 eyedroppers
pond water
2 slides with
   coverslips

microscope
pencil
paper
tap water

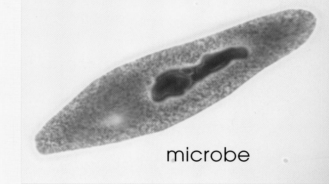

microbe

What You Do

1. With the eyedropper, place a drop of pond water on a slide.
2. Gently place a coverslip on top of the water drop.
3. Place the pond water slide on the microscope stage.
4. Look through the lens.
5. Count how many moving creatures you see through the lens. Write down the number you counted on a piece of paper.
6. Use a clean eyedropper to put a drop of tap water on a second slide. Place a coverslip on this water drop.
7. Place the tap water slide on the stage and look at it through the microscope. Write down the number of creatures you see in this water.

Did you see any tiny creatures moving in either drop of water? Which water had more microbes?

Amazing But True!

A microscope is an important tool during brain surgery. It allows a surgeon to make a smaller opening in the patient's head. The microscope also helps the surgeon guide a laser to remove tumors.

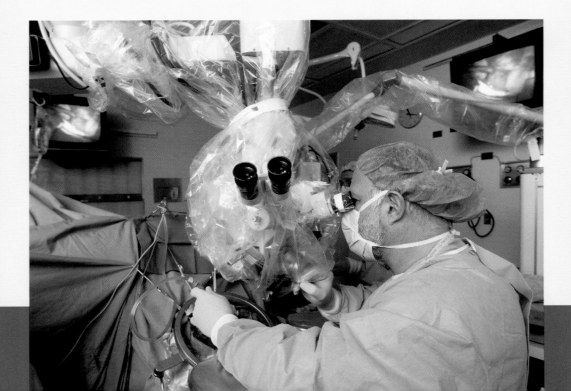

What Do You Think?

1. The parts of a microscope work together to show a larger image of a small object. Why is the lamp an important part of the microscope?

2. Some things that look the same to our eyes look different under a microscope. Can you think of some things that look different under a microscope?

3. Microscopes help people get a closer look at small objects. Can you think of some jobs where people use microscopes at work?

4. Microscopes have different kinds of lenses. What is one similarity and one difference between objective lenses and eyepiece lenses?

Glossary

eyepiece lens (EYE-peess LENZ)—a curved piece of glass in a microscope that magnifies an image from the objective lens

fiber (FYE-bur)—a long, thin thread of material, such as cotton, wool, or silk

magnify (MAG-nih-fye)—to make something look larger than it really is

microbe (MYE-krobe)—a living thing that is too small to see without a microscope

objective lens (uhb-JEK-tiv LENZ)—a curved piece of glass in a microscope that collects light and magnifies an image

slide (SLIDE)—a small piece of glass that holds objects so they can be seen under a microscope

stage (STAYJ)—a platform on a microscope that holds a slide

Read More

Bullock, Linda. *Looking through a Microscope.* Rookie Read-About Science. New York: Children's Press, 2003.

Kramer, Stephen P. *Hidden Worlds: Looking through a Scientist's Microscope.* Scientists in the Field. Boston: Houghton Mifflin, 2001.

Internet Sites

FactHound offers a safe, fun way to find Internet sites related to this book. All of the sites on FactHound have been researched by our staff.

Here's how:
1. Visit *www.facthound.com*
2. Type in this special code **0736825177** for age-appropriate sites. Or enter a search word related to this book for a more general search.
3. Click on the **Fetch It** button.

FactHound will fetch the best sites for you!

Index